GREAT SALT LAKE

GREAT SALT LAKE

A PERSPECTIVE FROM THE CHURCH OF JESUS CHRIST OF LATTER-DAY SAINTS

Bishop W. Christopher Waddell

THE UNIVERSITY OF UTAH PRESS
Salt Lake City

Publication of this edition is made possible in part by The Wallace Stegner Center for Land, Resources and the Environment, S. J. Quinney College of Law and by The Tanner Trust Fund, Special Collections Department, J. Willard Marriott Library

This lecture was originally delivered on March 17, 2023, at the 28th annual symposium of the Wallace Stegner Center for Land, Resources and the Environment. The symposium is supported by the R. Harold Burton Foundation, the founding and lead donor since 1996, and by the Cultural Vision Fund and The Nature Conservancy.

The Defiance House Man colophon is a registered trademark of the University of Utah Press. It is based on a four-foot-tall Ancient Puebloan pictograph (late PIII) near Glen Canyon, Utah.

LIBRARY OF CONGRESS CATALOGING-IN-PUBLICATION DATA
Names: Waddell, W. Christopher, (Wayne Christopher), 1959- author. |
    University of Utah. Wallace Stegner Center for Land, Resources and the
    Environment. Annual Symposium (28th : 2023 : Salt Lake City, Utah)
Title: Great Salt Lake : a perspective from the Church of Jesus Christ
    of Latter-day Saints / Bishop W. Christopher Waddell.
Identifiers: LCCN 2023045674 | ISBN 9781647691608 (paperback) | ISBN
    9781647691615 (ebook)
Subjects: LCSH: Water conservation--Utah--Great Salt Lake. | Water demand
    management--Utah--Great Salt Lake. | Environmental
    management--Utah--Great Salt Lake. | Water--Religious aspects--Church of
    Jesus Christ of Latter-day Saints. | Great Salt Lake (Utah)
Classification: LCC TD388 .W245 2023 | DDC 333.91/16--dc23/eng/20240110
LC record available at https://lccn.loc.gov/2023045674

Cover photo: *The Great Salt Lake* by Jonathan Cook-Fisher on Flikr (CC BY).
Errata and further information on this and other titles available at UofUpress.com.
Printed and bound in the United States of America.

Foreword

The Wallace Stegner Lecture serves as a public forum for addressing the critical environmental issues that confront society. Conceived in 2009 on the centennial of Wallace Stegner's birth, the lecture honors the Pulitzer Prize–winning author, educator, and conservationist by bringing a prominent scholar, public official, advocate, or spokesperson to the University of Utah with the aim of informing and promoting public dialogue over the relationship between humankind and the natural world. The lecture is delivered in connection with the Wallace Stegner Center's annual symposium and published by the University of Utah Press to ensure broad distribution. Just as Wallace Stegner envisioned a more just and sustainable world, the lecture acknowledges Stegner's enduring conservation legacy by giving voice to "the geography of hope" that he evoked so eloquently throughout his distinguished career.

Robert B. Keiter, Director
WALLACE STEGNER CENTER FOR LAND,
RESOURCES AND THE ENVIRONMENT

Great Salt Lake is one of the nation's true natural landmarks and an important resource for our community since 1847, and for the Native peoples before that—as visible and important as the Wasatch Mountains, breathtaking forests, and majestic red rock monuments.

On behalf of the Church of Jesus Christ of Latter-day Saints, I am also grateful to add our voice to what was shared today along with others who are engaged in the ongoing dialogue regarding the challenges we face and the solutions that are needed. Bishop Gérald Caussé, the Presiding Bishop of the Church of Jesus Christ of Latter-day Saints, presented an address titled "Our Earthly Stewardship" in the church's semi-annual General Conference in October last year. Speaking to millions of people worldwide, Bishop Caussé taught, "The care of the earth and of our natural environment is a sacred responsibility entrusted to us by God, which should fill us with a deep sense of duty and humility. It is also an integral component of our discipleship."[1]

Just days after General Conference, Bishop L. Todd Budge, Second Counselor in the Presiding Bishopric, delivered a message on environmental stewardship at the "Why It Matters" conference highlighting the United Nation's Sustainable Development Goals held at Utah Valley University. Bishop Budge said, "When it comes to taking care of the earth, we cannot afford to think only of today." He continued, "The consequences of our actions, for better or worse, accumulate into the future and are sometimes felt only generations later. Stewardship requires feet and hands at work in the present with a gaze fixed on the future."[2] He then shared various ways the church is striving to holistically improve its wise stewardship of natural resources, including agricultural land management, energy management, waste reduction, transportation, building practices and, most relevant to our topic today, water conservation.

Figure 1. Great Salt Lake

HISTORICAL EFFORTS

The Latter-day Saints' story in the Great Basin began in July 1847 with the first company of pioneers. As Apostle Wilford Woodruff entered the Salt Lake Valley, he was deeply impressed with what he saw. Especially notable to him was the "large lake of salt water" that stretched before his eyes.[3] The pioneers entered a region where Native American groups such as the Ute, the Paiute, and the Shoshone had managed water resources for hundreds of years.

Because of reports from earlier explorers, the Saints understood that rain alone was not sufficient to water crops in the arid Great Basin. They would need to draw from the streams, rivers, and lakes, following the example of Native Americans and Hispanic settlers that came before them. Almost immediately after reaching the valley floor, the pioneers built a diversion dam on what would become known as City Creek and dug a ditch so that water from the stream could soak the ground for crop cultivation.[4]

Over the next several decades, Latter-day Saint leaders helped communities construct irrigation networks that brought water to fields and enabled agricultural production. The Saints became

Figure 2. Irrigation

known for irrigation innovations and their ability to construct works that supplied water to vast expanses of land—stemming from their desire to be wise stewards and not waste this precious resource.[5] In an 1865 meeting with congregations from Box Elder and Cache Counties, Brigham Young taught, "We should waste nothing, but make everything in some way or other minister to our wants and independence."[6] Although today there are times when water needs to be conserved even if it could be used beneficially, Brigham Young believed that beneficial use reflected responsible stewardship over water. He also advocated for water to be held as a public resource and not in private ownership—a "radical" notion "by the standards of mid-nineteenth-century America," according to historian Donald Worster.[7]

The perspective of water as a community resource shifted over time as more settlers moved into Utah Territory and as the church itself became increasingly removed from farming and irrigation. Indeed, although the church still owns and operates some agricultural properties in Utah, this represents less than three percent of agricultural land in the state. The nineteenth-century Saints continued to view rivers, streams, and lakes as important and valuable

Figure 3. Salt Harvest

Figure 4. Recreation

resources—and not just meant for irrigation. Great Salt Lake's brackish waters, for instance, were valuable in their own right.

In the late-nineteenth and early-twentieth centuries, the church operated the Inland Crystal Salt Company that extracted salt from the lake and sold it throughout the American West. It also became involved in promoting recreation in Great Salt Lake.

The church helped found the Saltair Beach Company in 1891, and Saltair became a popular destination for locals and visitors alike.[8] Aside from the aesthetic of the lake that Wilford Woodruff

Figure 5. Early Twentieth-Century Meetinghouse

found so pleasing in 1847, the lake had become a useful resource for the church—and for everyone living in Utah.

In 1937 a big change took place, as the Improvement and Beautification Committee was established under the Welfare Program of the church to recommend landscaping practices for church members and church buildings, including the planting of lawns.

The idea in the United States that well-maintained lawns were a desirable component of landscaping stemmed from the mid-nineteenth century. Originally, only wealthy Americans with large manor estates had lawns, but after the Civil War they became "a status symbol of the middle class." A proliferation of lawns occurred in the twentieth century, especially after golf grew in popularity in the 1920s.[9]

Acting on these larger trends, the Improvement and Beautification Committee promoted the planting of lawns at the church's chapels. Church leaders approved of this practice in part because they wanted meetinghouse grounds to look clean and beautiful in preparation for the 1947 centennial celebration of the arrival of the pioneers to the Salt Lake Valley. "The appearance of Church and community buildings and homes," the First Presidency declared, "mirrors the pride and industry of a people."[10]

In more recent years, the impact that caring for these lawns could have on water supplies has become more apparent. When drought affected Utah and other western states at the turn of the twenty-first century, the Presiding Bishopric implemented conservation measures for the watering of church lawns, including a 25 percent reduction in the amount of water used for landscaping and recommending the use of higher mower settings so that grass could retain more moisture.[11]

CURRENT EFFORTS

In addition to steps we can take, individually and collectively, we also believe in a higher power that can be called upon. In an official statement made in June last year on the importance of water conservation, the church invited its members to "join with friends of other faiths in prayer to our Heavenly Father for rain and respite from the devasting drought," emphasizing that "we all play a part in preserving the critical resources needed to sustain life—especially water—and we invite others to join us in reducing water use wherever possible."[12] As the apostle James teaches us in the New Testament, we must show our "faith by [our] works" for "faith, if it hath not works, is dead."[13]

Though our efforts have not been and are still not perfect, there is a continual and ongoing church-wide effort to improve our care of natural resources, including the implementation of best practices

Figures 6 (top) and 7 (bottom): Traditional vs. Reduced Lawn

and available technology to improve our water efficiency. Let me share a few of the steps that are being taken, which we believe will make a difference.

On our farm properties, we have installed soil moisture probes to inform irrigation decisions and implementation of drip irrigation and micro-jet irrigation systems for appropriate crops. We perform regular maintenance and replace irrigation nozzles to maintain uniform water coverage. We individually tailor center pivot irrigation system programming to apply water at a variable rate based on soil types and observed low areas, and we are currently developing water management plans for all of our agricultural properties.

We have installed and continue to install smart controllers, hydrometers, rain sensors, and drip irrigation systems across our many meetinghouses, temples, and other facilities, and are encouraged to see positive impacts from these efforts. For example, from 2018 through the end of 2022, we saved nearly 40 million gallons of water each year at church headquarters. We are grateful for the diligent efforts of employees who monitor our irrigation systems and indoor plumbing, cooling, and other systems, and whose efforts have identified opportunities to improve our water efficiency.

In the early 2000s, the Meetinghouse Facilities Department began to adapt meetinghouse landscape standards by eco-regions within the state to better incorporate water-wise principles of regionally appropriate plant material accompanied by a reduction of lawns. This meant a transition away from more traditional landscaping which included 80 to 90 percent lawn towards a standard of 35 to 40 percent lawn for landscapes at new meetinghouses, incorporating more water-wise grass species and plant varieties.

Our current water-wise management plan also includes specific practices for pre-growing, growing, and post-growing seasons. These practices include the implementation and monitoring of irrigation systems, adjustment of irrigation controls to comply with water restrictions and weather, delaying first watering as long as possible, and applying water-saving products to lawn areas such as wetting agents and surfactants. The last item is actually the primary reason why some of our lawns maintain their green appearance despite reductions in water usage.

In 2022, as a result of these many efforts, water use at our Salt Lake County meetinghouses was reduced by 35 percent compared

Figure 8. BYU Campus

with 2020. We are grateful to our contractors, facility managers, and local leaders who have helped us in this effort. Once again, we acknowledge that our efforts are not perfect, and we invite church and community members to contact local church leadership if they observe instances where best practices are not adhered to. We urge local church leaders to be watchful stewards and report any concerns to church headquarters to ensure that our intended water management practices are appropriately executed.

Looking beyond church Headquarters and Salt Lake County, we are grateful for the many efforts being made on the BYU campus in Provo, Utah, to reduce water consumption. In the past two decades, the university has reduced its culinary water use by two-thirds, even as its building footprint has grown. Outdoors, BYU conducts regular water audits and uses smart irrigation systems and water-wise landscaping, including drought-tolerant plants and mulch made of campus green waste—food scraps, grass clippings, and wood chips. This mulch reduces water usage in flower and shrub beds by 30 percent. In response to heightened water concerns over the last decade, most of BYU's campus is now watered using secondary sources. The water master monitors stream flows and reduces flows, depending on conditions, by as little as 20 percent

Figure 9. Wise Stewardship

in spring to as much as 100 percent in late summer. As needed, campus lawns go dormant during dry spells. Additionally, on and off campus, BYU faculty contribute research on sustainable water supply, farming, and Great Salt Lake.[14]

In addition to "water-wise" efforts, in 2022 the church established a Sustainability Office and Sustainability Leadership Committee under the direction of the Presiding Bishopric to develop key cross-functional initiatives within church operations. We have expanded our teaching of the guiding principle of wise stewardship to emphasize the need to care for our natural resources and encourage our global employees to lead out in their efforts to implement creative solutions within the church's operations that "protect the future for all God's children."[15]

FUTURE ACTIONS

Our ability to be wise stewards of the earth is dependent on our understanding of the natural resources we have been blessed with. As our understanding of the environment grows, so does our

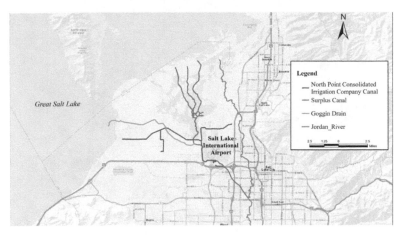

Figure 10. Map of NPCIC Donation Area

opportunity to align our practices with the environmental realities we face, allowing for the implementation of practical and effective localized solutions. We are indebted to the subject matter experts who study the conditions of Great Salt Lake and the impacts and future risks of its declining water levels. We are grateful for the legislative changes that create new opportunities to benefit the lake and to the many organizations working to bring awareness to this issue. With greater understanding of the lake and the solutions needed to help preserve it, we are positioned to improve our stewardship of this critical resource.

We are committed to be a part of the solution to help Great Salt Lake and have made some initial efforts to contribute. As was recently announced in a press release by the Utah Department of Natural Resources, the church has donated water shares in the North Point Consolidated Irrigation Company that will preserve in perpetuity a significant amount of water currently flowing to the lake.[16] This donation is believed to be the largest, permanent donation of water to benefit Great Salt Lake ever received by the state. The shares provide approximately 20,000 acre-feet or up to 50 cubic feet per second of water that is equivalent to the amount of water for 20,000 single family home connections. This donation will also

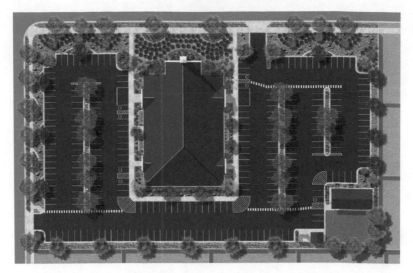

Figure 11. Drought-tolerant plants and trees on a design for a meetinghouse in Vineyard, Utah.

help preserve critical shoreline and wetland habitat in Farmington Bay. We are happy to support the state's plans to improve water measurement and management, and hope this will facilitate and encourage future similar transactions.

In accordance with HB-33 passed last year, we are also conducting an evaluation to identify other church-owned water assets that can feasibly be delivered to Great Salt Lake—a continuation of our efforts that began in 2021. As a first priority, we are evaluating the water assets within the five counties surrounding Great Salt Lake as well as water assets diverted from Utah Lake which we expect will have the highest likelihood of successful delivery to the lake. We know that every bit helps, and we invite other water asset owners to consider the new opportunities afforded by recent legislative changes and determine how they might help in this important effort. We thank the Utah Department of Natural Resources and its Divisions of Water Rights, Forestry Fire and State Lands, and Wildlife Resources; The Nature Conservancy and National Audubon Society, co-managers of Great Salt Lake Watershed Enhancement Trust; and subject matter

Figure 12. Aerial View of COB Plaza

experts from Brigham Young University, Utah State University, and others who have met and consulted with our internal teams.

Beyond the state of Utah, and as part of our long-term water conservation plans, we are making a concerted effort to extend water-wise practices churchwide, including expanding our use of technology, water management plans, and other best practices. We will continue to incorporate water-wise and sustainable landscaping principles at our new meetinghouses and temples along the Wasatch Front, such as the use of native or adapted drought-tolerant plants and trees as is demonstrated by the landscape design rendering in figure 11 for a future meetinghouse in Vineyard, Utah.

However, on a larger scale, our aim is to understand more fully what sustainable landscaping should be based on local climates and identify opportunities to conserve water and natural resources. This includes improving runoff water quality, collecting and re-using stormwater, mitigating the heat island effect, and integrating the landscape into the existing and regional context. We are currently working with landscape architects that are well-versed in these sustainability landscape principles and recommendations from programs such as LEED and Sustainable SITES Initiatives as part of a retrofit pilot for select meetinghouses across the state.

Figure 13. COB Plaza Plants

We are very excited that many of these sustainable landscaping principles are incorporated into our landscape upgrades for Temple Square and downtown Headquarters properties. For example, we are implementing climate-based evapotranspiration smart controllers so our irrigation schedule will be influenced by real-time weather conditions, and we have grouped plants of like water requirements in hydro-zones to further improve our watering efficiency.

Just a few years ago, in 2019, we began developing our water management strategy for new construction and retrofitting existing plants and soils. Our soils were chosen and engineered for water- and nutrient-holding capacity. All of our trees, shrubs, and perennial beds are watered via micro-irrigation methods and were selected for their low water-use characteristics.

Future visitors to Temple Square will notice some key changes including more trees, less grass, and more perennial plants. Our new tree count will be increased by 30 percent to reduce the heat island effect and to establish tree canopies that will protect the plants below and reduce our HVAC cooling of surrounding build-ings. Our turfgrass on the other hand has been reduced by 35 percent and our annuals reduced by 50 percent. We have also executed a turfgrass summer dormancy program in which all turfgrass will

Figure 14. Full View of COB Plaza

receive 35-40 percent less irrigation water from June to September.

With all these changes, we estimate that in the first five years as the landscape is being established, the total estimated water savings will be 40-50 million gallons from our pre-construction amounts. Once established, we estimate an additional 15-20 million gallons will be saved annually from those same pre-construction amounts. As President Russell M. Nelson stated in his General Conference address in October 2021 regarding the Salt Lake City temple renovations, "It is now time that we each implement extraordinary measures—perhaps measures we have never taken before—to strengthen our personal spiritual foundations. Unprecedented times call for unprecedented measures."[17] We are grateful for President Nelson's wise and optimistic call for continuous improvement in our spiritual lives and believe his words can be a clear guide for our efforts to be wise stewards as well.

CONCLUSION

As the church strives to reduce its water use, we invite members of the church and community to also reduce their consumption. We encourage engagement and responsiveness to legislative changes and other recommendations from subject matter experts recognizing the need to act with urgency and unity towards the future we hope for—one with a healthy Great Salt Lake.

I echo the invitation given last June for all to pray and fast for "rain and respite from the devasting drought" and for inspiration to know how we can each individually contribute to a resolution of this difficult issue.[18]

As the Lord taught the children of Israel in Leviticus 26, "If ye walk in my statutes, and keep my commandments, and do them; then I will give you rain in due season, and the land shall yield her increase, and the trees of the field shall yield their fruit."[19]

We are grateful for the snow and rain we have received this season—though perhaps not when we are shoveling our driveways. We should acknowledge God's hands in providing us this blessing *and* that our work is not done yet. We must continue with all diligence if we are to make the difference that is needed. May the Lord grant us all the faith and perseverance to be wise stewards of our water, our land, and the resources that flow through them.

Notes

1.   Bishop Gérald Caussé, "Our Earthly Stewardship," General Conference, October 2022.

2.   Bishop L. Todd Budge, "Our Sacred Duty to Care for the Earth," Church Newsroom, October 5, 2022.

3.   Wilford Woodruff, "Journal (January 1, 1847 – December 31, 1853)," July 24, 1847, The Wilford Woodruff Papers, accessed January 18, 2023, https://wilfordwoodruffpapers.org/p/YE92.

4.   Howard Stansbury, *An Expedition to the Valley of the Great Salt Lake in Utah* (London: Sampson, Low, Son Lippincott, Grambo & Co, 1852), 140; Thomas G. Alexander, "Interdependence and Change: Mutual Irrigation Companies in Utah's Wasatch Oasis in an Age of Modernization, 1870-1930," *Utah Historical Quarterly* 71 (Fall 2003): 292.

5.   George Thomas, *The Development of Institutions Under Irrigation with Special Reference to Early Utah Conditions* (New York: The MacMillan Company, 1920), 13-14.

6.   Brigham Young, August 1-10, 1865, *Journal of Discourses*, 11:129-30.

7. Donald J. Worster, *Rivers of Empire: Water, Aridity, and the Growth of the American West* (New York: Pantheon Books, 1985), 78.

8. James E. Talmage, *The Great Salt Lake: Past and Present* (Salt Lake City: Deseret News, 1900), 35.

9. Virginia Scott Jenkins, *The Lawn: A History of an American Obsession* (Washington, DC: Smithsonian Institution Press, 1994), 3-5, 14.

10. As quoted in "Our Chapels and Homes Shall Be Beautiful," CR 35 1, box 1, folder 4, Church History Library, Church of Jesus Christ of Latter-day Saints, Salt Lake City, Utah (CHL).

11. The Presiding Bishopric to Building Managers in Utah, Idaho, Nevada, Arizona, and California, September 4, 2001, CR 4 205, box 12, CHL.

12. "The Importance of Water Conservation," *Church News*, June 22, 2022, https://newsroom.churchofjesuschrist.org/article/drought-water-conservation-statement.

13. James 2:17-18, KJV New Testament.

14. Kayson M. Shurtz, Emily Dicataldo, Robert B. Sowby, and Gustavious P. Williams, "Insights into Efficient Irrigation of Urban Landscapes: Analysis Using Remote Sensing, Parcel Data, Water Use, and Tiered Rates," *Sustainability* 14, no. 3 (January 26, 2022): 1427. https://doi.org/10.3390/su14031427; Brittany Karford Rogers, "When in Drought: Thoughts from BYU Experts," *Y Magazine*, 2022. https://magazine.byu.edu/article/when-in-drought-utah/.

15. M. Russell Ballard, "Children of Heavenly Father," BYU Speeches, March 3, 2020. https://speeches.byu.edu/talks/m-russell-ballard/children-heavenly-father/.

16. Utah Department of Natural Resources, "Church Donates Water to the State of Utah to Benefit Great Salt Lake," March 16, 2023, https://naturalresources.utah.gov/dnr-newsfeed/church-donates-water-to-benefit-great-salt-lake.

17. President Russell M. Nelson, "The Temple and Your Spiritual Foundation," General Conference, October 2021. https://www.churchofjesuschrist.org/study/general-conference/2021/10/47nelson?lang=eng.

18. "The Importance of Water Conservation," *Church News*, June 22, 2022, https://newsroom.churchofjesuschrist.org/article/drought-water-conservation-statement.

19. Leviticus 26:3-4, KJV Old Testament.

About the Author

Bishop W. Christopher Waddell was named First Counselor in the Presiding Bishopric of the Church of Jesus Christ of Latter-day Saints on October 3, 2020. He was named a General Authority Seventy, and served in that capacity until his call as Second Counselor in the Presiding Bishopric. Bishop Waddell received a bachelor's degree from San Diego State University and worked with Merrill Lynch in several positions, including first vice president of investments. Bishop Waddell has served in numerous church callings, including full-time missionary in Spain, bishop, high councilor, counselor in a mission presidency, stake president, president of the Spain Barcelona Mission, and Area Seventy. He is married to Carol Stansel and they are the proud parents of four children.